DUCK Fever

DUCK HUNTING CARTOONS

by Bruce Cochran

Willow Creek Press

Copyright ©1992 by Bruce Cochran

Published by
Willow Creek Press
An imprint of NorthWord Press, Inc.
Box 1360, Minocqua, WI 54548

ISBN 1-55971-183-3

For information on other Willow Creek
titles, write or call 1-800-336-5666.

Designed by Russell S. Kuepper
Printed in the U.S.A.

Library of Congress Cataloging-in-Publication Data

Cochran, Bruce.
    Duck fever : duck hunting cartoons / by Bruce Cochran.
        p.   cm.
    ISBN 1-55971-183-3 : $12.50 -- ISBN 1-55971-182-5 : $7.95
    1. Duck shooting--Caricatures and cartoons   2. American wit and
humor, Pictorial. I. Title.
NC1429.C619A4 1992
741.5'973--dc20
                                                            92-27586
                                                            CIP

For Ned

ABOUT THE FEVERED MIND
OF BRUCE COCHRAN

Cartoonist Bruce Cochran brings his humor to us from a broad background in the outdoors as well as the arts.

Graduating from Oklahoma University with his Bachelor's in Design, he worked for Hallmark Cards as a writer/illustrator, and soon moved on to freelancing jobs with such publications as *Playboy*, *Look*, *Saturday Evening Post*, *Sports Afield*, *Field & Stream* and the nation's #1 selling newspaper, *USA Today*. His previous cartoon collections for Willow Creek Press include *Buck Fever* and *Bass Fever*.

His interest in the outdoors makes Cochran an avid hunter, fisherman, and collector of antique duck decoys. A sponsor member of Ducks Unlimited, his watercolors have been exhibited at the Easton, MD Waterfowl Festival and the National Ducks Unlimited Wildlife Art Show, among others.

Cochran is married to his wife of 33 years, has two children and has, he says, "been trained by a succession of three Labrador retrievers."

6

"It's not a dictionary. It's this year's waterfowl regulations."

"Pintails are a no-no, Canvasbacks are 100 points. Gadwall, teal, and widgeons are twenty points.
It's ok to shoot one mallard hen but they really wish you wouldn't. The north zone opens October 20th
and closes November 1st. In the east zone you can shoot two bonus scaup on Thursdays.
The south zone opens November 26th except in Area B, where it opens December 1st. Any questions?"

"With today's seasons and bag limits, we've loaded enough shells to last 247 years."

"Here's the plan: We stay up north as long as we can, then migrate at night
and raft up in the middle of big lakes during the day."

"It's not just brown, sir. It's Mud Camo!"

"I've never seen your dad so anxious for duck season."

"I've got electric socks, insulated waders, expedition-weight polypropylene underwear, a polar fleece shirt, and a Gore-Tex / Thinsulate parka!! What the hell do you mean it's going to be 75 and sunny?!?"

"Don't forget tomorrow is opening day."

"Remind me never to hunt a public area opening day again."

"Dogs fighting, the smell of scorched coffee, duck calls piercing the morning stillness. I LOVE opening day!"

"There's nothing like being out here in polypropylene underwear, polar fleece pants, and Gore-Tex / Thinsulate coats to really get a guy close to nature."

"Man! I was getting claustrophobia! I had to get out of the house for a while!"

"You've got your Federal Duck Stamp and your State Duck Stamp,
but you don't have a **county** stamp and I don't see a building permit for your blind."

"Those guys behind us are the lousiest callers I've ever heard."

"What kind of call did you say that was?"

"No wonder we've got this place all to ourselves!"

"It's the newest thing in camo. It's called 'Lakeside Litter.'"

"Maybe we've got our decoys arranged wrong."

"Listen! I hear a wounded cow!"

"You don't mind if we listen to this duck calling instruction tape for a couple of hours, do you?"

"It's my favorite print. It's called 'Mallards Over Wild Rice.'"

"You pooped it. You scoop it."

"Admit it! You ate my goose call!"

"Whaddaya mean 'another duck print??' These are **geese**!!"

"And you call yourself a retriever!"

*"Why can't you just lay around **in front** of the fireplace like the dogs in the magazines?"*

29

"Which way is south?"

"Look, dad! A married duck!"

"OK! It was a lousy shot! Your last retrieve was nothing to brag about either, you know!"

"Don't tell mom we won a puppy 'til after I've fixed her a drink."

"They'll teach you all that stuff about obedience and retrieving. **I'll** teach you the **important** stuff like how to get a doughnut out of a coat pocket and how to scare the hell out of a postman."

"That'll be $20 for the shots, $15 for worming, and $2,000 to remodel my office."

DOG TRAINING EQUIPMENT

WHISTLE

DUMMY

COLLAR

LEASH

CHECK CORD

CHAIR

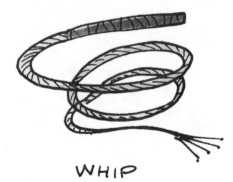

WHIP

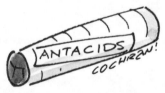

ANTACIDS
(FOR TRAINER)

"... insulated chest waders, a Gore-Tex parka, and ... just a second ..."

"This is the last time I ever take **you** to the grocery store with me!"

"Relax! The book says he'll calm down by the time he's two."

"You've **got** to make him stop drinking out of the toilet! Especially when I'm sitting on it!"

"Quick! Let's watch this training video before he eats the T.V. set!"

TEACH
YOUR DOG TO
HEEL
IN 10 YEARS

"When I say 'come,' dammit, you **will** come!"

"Isn't that the guy up the street whose yard the pup always poops in?"

"You don't think I'm spoiling him, do you?"

"Did dad name the pup 'Dammit'?"

"Dear Dog Supplies Inc: The electric collar doesn't even faze him. Do you make a nuclear collar?"

*"Not bad for your first retrieve. Now try it with a **duck**."*

"Not now, dammit! I'll tell you when!"

"When he finishes my sandwich, will he eat my shotgun shells?"

"It comes with a detachable head so you can turn the body over and use it for a canoe."

*"I thought they just **nested** in wash tubs."*

*"I did things like this in the army, but someone was **making** me do it!"*

"I'll set the alarm for eight A.M. That's when the first flight usually comes in."

"I just hope a bull doesn't come along before we limit out."

"Keep calling! He's getting closer!"

"I told you that goose was too big for the pup!"

"Snow goose at eleven o'clock!"

"So I says to her, 'You won't be seeing much of me for a while.
This time of year I spend every weekend out in the bay on my yacht!'"

"Ouch! I just bit down on a steel shot pellet!"

"Let's get as far away from these guys as possible."

"Come on in. They're all asleep."

"Big deal. I've got a down vest, and it didn't cost me $57.95, either."

"In the magazines they always drop gracefully into the decoys with their wings cupped."

"No, No! Not now! Wait 'til he's heading for the woods with a roll of toilet paper!"

"Are you sure the magazine said you could build a duck blind on **any** boat?"

"I thought they **flew** south for the winter!"

"I see the big rednecks have finally come down!"

"Like my new tires? I found 'em hanging on a fence post."

"When Uncle Charlie blows it, it sounds like a goose. When I blow it, it sounds like a school bus."

"1987! That was a good year for bluebills!"

". . . and before Buster I had Old Nell . . . five dogs ago? . . . no, six.
Anyway, Old Nell could retrieve all day! Why, I remember one time . . ."

"I've got a great fund raising idea for D.U.!
We put all my recipes in a cook book and . . . what the hell's the matter?"

"It's amazing what Uncle Charlie can do with three mergansers and a little hot sauce, isn't it?"

"You think this is bad?! You should've been out here in the big storm of '52! . . ."

. . . It was so cold I had to stuff my dog down inside my long-johns to save his life! . . .

. . . The big red legs had just come down and their legs all turned **blue**! . . .

*. . . A penguin walked by on the ice and he was **shivering**! . . .*

. . . I had to set fire to my beard to keep my face from gettin' frostbit! . . .

*. . . I would've froze to death but I shot a goose, gutted him, and crawled inside the cavity to keep warm!
Did I ever tell you about that goose? That goose was **so big** . . ."*

"I carved these decoys myself, kid! With a chain saw!"

"They ain't really boots anymore, kid. They're mostly just patches held together with duct tape."

"Good news and bad news, kid. The good news is, I've got your breakfast ready.
The bad news is, it's left-over bufflehead drumstick and a warm beer."

"He may not be hungry. He ate two decoys and a roll of duct tape this morning."

"My shotgun is an 'over-and-over,' kid. I have to pump it over and over to make it work."

"If we get close enough to the water before we get stuck, we can hunt out of the jeep!"

"In this fog they could be right on top of us and we'd never know it."

"Try some of my muskrat jerky, kid. But don't eat too much. You'll get a hair ball."

"Duck hunting teaches you to deal with problems you'll face later in life, kid. Like boredom, for instance."

"When I said you had to have a plug in your gun, I didn't mean a plug of **tobacco**!"

"See, kid? You gotta shoot where they ain't even at yet."

"If the wind's out of the north, we'll hunt the point blind . . .

. . . if we get a west wind and it rains, the south blind should be good. If it snows, we hunt the cornfield blind . . .

. . . if it floods, we'll take the boat and hunt the timber. An earthquake will give the decoys lots of action, in which case we'll hunt the big lake. If a volcano erupts, we'll hunt the lava flows 'til the decoys catch fire!"

*"What Uncle Charlie's trying to say is that we're hunting tomorrow, no matter **what**!"*

"*Another good thing about my Gadwall Gumbo, kid. What we don't eat we can patch the boat with.*"

"I ever tell you about the time I was cleaning out a wood duck house and found a six-foot blacksnake inside?"

"I see the big redlegs have finally come down."

"We call this 'The Elvis Blind.'"

"Save your beer bottles. Uncle Charlie reloads."

"Uncle Charlie sent you his favorite duck recipe:
'Poke stick up duck's butt and roast over campfire 'til you're drunk enough to eat it.'"

"We haven't seen a duck in two hours. Think I'll get out and stretch my legs."

"Decoys are interesting as folk art, but I could never become physically attracted to one."

"The red-winged blackbird attachment comes extra."

"We could have pulled that flock in if we'd had more decoys."

"I wish some new ducks would come down. These birds have been looking at decoys all season."

"You'd never get away with that if I had a shotgun in my hand instead of a coffee cup!"

"Whaddaya mean, 'Keep your head down'?
With all this stuff hanging around my neck, I couldn't stick my head up if I wanted to!"

"The only way I like ice is in a glass with whiskey poured over it."

"We'll never know if we get hypothermia! We're **always** uncoordinated and unable to think clearly!"

"See? All these years you thought I was out here enjoying myself."

"I think you nicked him."

"Ever get the feeling they know when shooting hours are over?"

"He's hell on divers."

"According to this banding information, the duck you shot was a little girl's pet.
He trusted people and readily came to you because he expected you to feed him."

"Hey! That lonesome hen call really works!"

"I've heard of oversized decoys, but **this** is ridiculous!"